Tell It Like It Might Be

To Nancy with much love and many thanks

Tell It Like It Might Be
Michael Bartholomew-Biggs

Published 2008 by
Smokestack Books
PO Box 408, Middlesbrough TS5 6WA
e-mail : info@smokestack-books.co.uk
www.smokestack-books.co.uk

Tell It Like It Might Be
Michael Bartholomew-Biggs
Copyright 2008

Printed by
EPW Print & Design Ltd

ISBN 978-0-9554028-4-5
Smokestack Books gratefully
acknowledges the support of
Middlesbrough Borough Council
and Arts Council North East

Smokestack Books is
represented by Inpress Ltd
www.inpressbooks.co.uk

LEEDS LIBRARIES AND INFORMATION SERVICE	
LD39594947	
HJ	07/11/2008
821.9	£7.95
S035179	

Some of these poems first appeared in *Inklings of Complicity* (Pikestaff Press 2003) and in *Acumen, Ambit, The Coffee House, Critical Survey, Envoi, Iota, Magma, Orbis, Other Poetry, Paging Doctor Jazz, The Rialto, River King Poetry Supplement (USA), The Rue Bella, Seam, The SHOp, Staple, Upstart* and *Ware Poetry Competition Anthology.*
Thanks also to the Cross Street poetry workshop.

Contents

- 9 St Thomas's First Miracle in India
- 10 The Otters Greet St Cuthbert
- 11 Islington Green
- 12 Tenacious Sugarbush
- 13 Uncommon Worship
- 14 Living Language
- 15 Stained Glass in Tudeley Church
- 16 Aviary in Dulwich Park
- 17 Out of Reach
- 18 Jairus
- 19 Dream Catching
- 20 Psychiatric Wing
- 21 Identity Crisis
- 22 Family Hotel
- 23 Moving Image
- 24 Eleventh Floor
- 25 Call this Fog?
- 26 Zone Two
- 28 Tell it Like it Might Have Been
- 30 Signals
- 31 Masquerade
- 32 Close Enough for Jazz
- 33 First Tango
- 34 Casting Off
- 35 Norwegian Wood
- 36 Atmospheres
- 37 Moonlight Masquerade
- 38 At the Caffé dell Tasso
- 40 Killing Time at the Flying-boat Museum
- 42 Loss Adjusters
- 43 So, What Happened?
- 44 Party Trick
- 45 Analysis
- 46 Curtain Call

- 47 Adultery-on-sea
- 48 Denunciation
- 49 Voice
- 50 Fault Lines
- 51 Tribe
- 53 Clips of Documentary Footage
- 54 Their Minds were Settled
- 55 Foreboding
- 56 Capital Offence
- 57 Cover Up
- 58 Fool's-errand Boys
- 59 To Whom it May Concern
- 60 Troubadours

- 61 Notes

St Thomas's First Miracle in India

First he showed them something obvious:
scooping palmfulls from this greater sea
than Galilee, he scattered them as shining
droplets that were swallowed up like seeds
in soil. 'Must they always fall?' he asked,
then answered, 'Not if my God gets there first.'

So they dared him with their smiling silence.
He threw two-handed, higher than before,
and as his faith flew upwards with the splash
they saw the water freeze in burning sunlight:
a broken ring, a crown of beads and shards,
a jagged halo hovered overhead.

No-one moved; but nothing stayed as still
as the impossible. A catechism
sketched itself: 'Will you reach out and hope
such water touches you? Or will you stand,
slack-armed, and watch the ocean take it back
shrugging with an old indifference?'

The Otters Greet St Cuthbert

In him it would be easier than most
for creatures to detect a wiry likeness,
earthy fragrance of Creator;

so they padded up the beach and curled
themselves about his shrivelled, salt-burned feet,
worshipping as well as warming;

and though they had no words for it, their need
of blessing was as real as any craving
ever met through taste or touch.

His voice caressed their ears and they slipped back
into the long sleek ocean, reassured
at being known for what they were.

Islington Green

for Graham Claydon

Unlike Lincoln,
this borough does not qualify a colour
for making up heroic doublets.

A passer-through
sees patchy tarmac, sooty bricks. Graffiti
daubs the church and round its porch

religious pigeons
peck second-hand confetti; but the steeple
would scarcely have to crane its neck

to get a sight
of honeysuckle camouflaging walls
and shrubs bunched plump in sunny corners.

Ivy claims
the drainpipes, brambles clamber over fences
and nettles, if there's nothing else,

make up the numbers
when leaves applaud the rain. Sometimes ducks
occur in unexpected places.

Unpromising,
yet filled with little promised lands: this parish
fashions parables with offshoots

of the tree
whose roots and stems assert themselves the same
in Eden and Gethsemane.

Tenacious Sugarbush

Just like flowers, someone says,
all the colours in one border.
Easy, from the footpath, to be charmed
and yet not see the single blooms.

In smells of sunshine, spice and dust
she's queuing, pregnant, in a cotton dress.
We're both voting is the joke
she tells the camera

with fresh-picked self-respect,
the kind that's faded in the buttonholes
of those who've never lacked the means
to take themselves for granted.

Now confidence is walking the long road
away from prison, waving, shaking hands
with strangers and admitting *maybe
it won't last, but now we're standing,*

being counted and we count. The words,
expansive as a fanfare, shape a smile
the way that *Protea tenax* petals
start unbending, taking their own time.

South Africa, April 1994

Uncommon Worship

Sudden from the unused church at noon
bursts a strangely urgent angelus.
One priestly function still persists
though delegated to electric motors:
chiming timely calls to prayer
across the empty fields to absent workers
and to me, on leave in Anhliac.

I mutter something as I start the car:
an automatic Grace, a half Our Father
offered as response. Caught out,
I'm open-mouthing like a puzzled fish
pulled from depths of murky water
into too-pure air; the words seem hollow
as the plastic icthys on the dash.

Warm and heavy scents of fresh-mown hay
are lingering like incense as I coast,
with windows open, down the hill,
the easy way towards the riverside
and lunch; I start imagining
the bruised-grass pepper taste of watercress
melting like a wafer on my tongue.

Living Language

CD-ROMs are whispering
in tongues beside me as we fill
the gallery to watch the wrestlers
do their best at pinning down
the Word of God across a canvas.

What they make me want to ask
is, did he say *Sono la via*,
sono la verita, la vita
in those Renaissance upper rooms?
And would those vowels have rung more truly
with his voice than John fourteen
verse six's English paraphrase
of half-remembered Aramaic?

There is another gift of tongues
apart from Pentecost: some truths,
as versatile as fire, ignite
whatever kindling sticks of language,
dry or green, they choose to burn.

National Gallery, April 2000

Stained Glass in Tudeley Church

for Rosy Fairhurst

Cool blues control the north and east.
Like cloths for washing perspiration,
they chill our motorway impatience,
retard my heart's too-rapid patter.
Yellows falling from south-west
are harsher: shades of golden calves
and gilded lilies, not the shining
head of Saint Veronica.

We've reached a vee of contradiction,
light that soothes and light that scolds;
so does it pay to deviate
from traffic in the obvious?
The walls, for all the history
of liturgy that clings to them
like candle grease, give no opinions.
The windows weigh the evidence

and tell us we don't walk on water
or build ladders to the sun.
When someone in the car-park asks
'Who knows the way to go from here?'
the answer only funnels us
past rival tinted images
in glass of malls and superstores
all promising a better deal.

And there I'd shrug and stop – except
I know you'd say we needn't scorn
life's special offers: like good friends,
good books and, yes, good wine and laughter;
like compassion which observes
a roughly-painted world through lenses
of pure colour, making even
poor approximations look like white.

Aviary in Dulwich Park

Whatever moves them
it is no concern of ours
propelling sudden flights, like streaks
escaping from a child's paintbrush,
on wingbeats measured to a space
as narrow as the span of our attention.

    We leave our son in hospital
    at two pm and there is just this park
    to walk in since we caught an early train
    for fear of being late we're here too soon
    not knowing either how to pass the time
    or any way to spin it out for ever.

We snatch at straws
to weave and moss with optimism
cushioning our fledgling hopes.
Bright flowers advertise survival
and the chattering of finches
sounds like the repetition of small prayers.

Out of Reach

Evening flung a flock of birds against the sky,
stretching like a net to catch the setting sun.
Obedient to inertia and the wind, it swirled
and fell back empty through itself to drape and settle
on a pair of trees whose canopies connected.

So bloody what? Dramatic images stay cheap
when owning real emotions starts to cost too much.

Knowing that tomorrow morning you'd be leaving,
we took a late and thoughtful walk along the towpath.
Our shoulders shared the backward drag of memories
while winds from up ahead disturbed the patient water,
chill or apprehension fretting it to gooseflesh.

Somewhere in our talk I said to you, *Take care*,
and you said, simply, *Yes*. Then when we held each other
with our eyes it seemed as though two radar beams
had locked upon a moment when our faithfulness
alone might be enough to keep your flight from harm

and to guide a surgeon's hands to guarantee
to catch and lift the shadow draped across your breast.

Jairus

Hired mourners always think that they know best:
and yet he got the better of them –
put them out of doors
and countenance, replacing grief with grievance
by making grief redundant.

After first delaying with that woman
he was firmly undelayed
by men whose bad-news faces
showed what they believed: to send for him
had been undignified

and vain as running circles round a fear
of how fears feel when they come true.
But which is worse? The pain?
Or practising a memory of pain
before the pain arrives?

Parents dare not think of knowing better
than the very worst there is
when there it is: a vase
once smashed, though showing half itself intact,
will stay forever empty.

Her fingers on the counterpane were stiff
as splinters. At his touch they curled
to clasp the hand that softened
brittle clay as you or I might melt
the wax that sealed a warrant.

Dream Catching

As we sat there watching by the bedside,
waiting for her wakening,
the flyscreen seemed to digitise the sky
and make the framed blue cloudy square
convincingly unreal,
like a Magritte postcard magnified.

> When dead people come into her dreams
> it's always raining. They arrive by horse
> and buggy, Jim and Mary sitting close
> with Harry driving. They're still young and laughing
> never mind the drizzle and the splashing
> wheels. Now George is there quite suddenly
> which makes the wagon tilt so all of them
> are thrown together. Mary shrieks and grabs
> at Jim; but George's arms are strong as well.
> The cart begins to gather too much speed,
> like falling more than flying. She's outside
> now, watching as disaster starts to tumble
> from the trestle bridge and more afraid
> of what her mind can show her than about
> her skin. For waking is the only way
> she knows of dying in a dream.

At any rate she's peaceful while she's sleeping
someone says and we accept
this interpretation with relief.
An icing-sugar coating settles
as our close-meshed wishes
sift away implausibilities.

Psychiatric Wing

Horrid corridors fly off at crazy angles.
'I don't want relationships:
not with anyone' insists a voice behind me,
nouns all bound in bandages.

Yasmin holds both stiffened arms close by her sides
to parallel her skirt's dark stripes;
in artificial stillness, like a stateless queen,
her eyes are locked upon the doctor.

Marianna shouts at random, playing parent
to her own unruly childhood;
strokes the silent wheelchaired girl's limp hand
to compensate her self for scoldings.

Steven, pacing on the spot to keep his place
in middle distance, prophesies
a peace – which is fulfilled when Eric ends his anger
transcribing Janine's spoken poem.

One evening an escape occurs among the rafters.
A bat flicks like a black crepe cut-out
across confining alcoves, blind to open windows.
No-one mentions metaphors.

Identity Crisis

Ghost stories do not usually begin
in hotel lavatories
even when they're euphemised
as shady-sounding *cloakrooms*.
An air of salty functionality
discourages the supernatural.

But it was while I dried my hands
a figure came from nowhere –
or a cubicle – and shouldered past
to beat me to the door.
Who was myself. And, when I saw this,
whom I chased along a corridor

towards a gilded mirror, holding up
a pair of shared reflections
(the other one was rather paler).
My voice was trapped inside my throat
but croaked an oath or feeble threat.
'Don't question me' the double said.

Then my late father entered, limping,
looking for his hat. 'Who do you see?'
I whisper-shouted and he smiled
but didn't answer – only held his arms out
to embrace the one who wasn't me
and wasn't me and wasn't me.

Family Hotel, Paris 1962

The wall beside the stairs was curved and green.
Back windows let in mottled smells from kitchens
far below the sky. A pair of sisters
from Ashby-de-la-Zouch left English papers
at my door. The quietest hour was always
shortly after dawn when lack of chatter
from the bar below awoke my need
to empty last night's wine – but not *en suite*

and, coming back, I missed my way. It was
as if another creature – not a servant
or a dog – pushed past me through a lightweight
glazed and varnished door onto a landing.
In a mirror by the early light
I saw a life-size portrait of Madame,
the founder's wife, bare-armed, Edwardian
black dress low-cut, white throat caressed by pearls.

I took her image back to bed and wrestled
sleep till morning. Then the landing door
had gone; the mirror's glass was cracked and time
had nibbled at its silvering. The picture
of Madame was missing but the same
sweet perfect-oval face acknowledged me
behind the desk where brochures lay in rows
like answers waiting for unspoken questions.

Moving Image

Her parcel gives the game away.
The Modigliani lady
with her arrow face and narrow shoulders
plainly is escaping from a painting.

Against her shabby black silk blouse
she carries carefully
a paper box in white with perfect corners.
It was wrapped for her, perhaps, in Arles

by that unknown confectioner
whose little girl, when grown,
would just recall Van Gogh as being grumpy
(evading every myth about the painter).

Not too obvious a voyeur,
I avoid her eyes
then catch her in each moment she approaches.
As we pass, I guess she'll have no thickness

and a back of empty canvas:
but, nimble as a fly-half,
she wrongfoots my fancies by being real
enough to step right through my frame of reference.

Braga, 1995

Eleventh Floor

Candy is my weakness.
The grey-pink wall around your high-rise balcony
yielded as my fancy pressed against it
like nougat to a tongue
and, stretching into sticky strands, it bulged

to tilt me slowly outwards
just before your grip upon the camera failed
at the instant when the shutter tripped
and it went plummeting
to photograph its own destruction

in a zoom lens shot
that ultimately missed the lady on the street
turning pirouettes as laboured as
a drowsy ballerina
or a skater in a space suit

who thought she was concealed
by sidewalk shrubs that altitude had simplified
to jumbles of brown smudges, just as if
the city's landscape artist
had rummaged in a box of chocolates.

Call This Fog?

Stamping to exaggerate the chill
we met each other one November night,
the four of us, the only four it seemed
who cared to make it to the reading.

'Call this fog?' I ventured stupidly
to break the ice. 'Why, I remember London
smogs were twice as thick, you couldn't see
a hand before your face and all you heard
were thuds as people dropped like flies.'

Later on we talked of the Dordogne
and Durham and we made them rhyme.

By next November only two survived,
partnerless in low speed desperation
of baffled butterflies escaping from
the vapour of a killing jar.

They walked a fog-damped night to find the station
where someone should arrive. The street lamps flared
like matches struck one-handed; buses tumbrilled
strange commuters; talking hid a need
to ask whose train would get in first.

Now there are travel tales from the Algarve
and Arles that they both know by heart.

Zone Two

At the station exit
a false proscenium arch reveals
and frames a square of late October.
Evening mist; a hint of coal-smoke mixed
with ozone off the District Line;
stage right, the railway embankment
uplit by a wash of sulphur yellow
from the candle-strip of lamps
that curves across the dusky park
towards a sky-glow from the glassworks;
disappearing in the distance
a schoolboy finishing a training run.

When the fogs were thicker,
bitter as a pack of acid drops,
figures would emerge on muffled steps
along the path just *there*
beside the see-saw, all of them
but one resolving into strangers.

Now I'm walking it again
and treading on the cracks; whatever
I thought threatening
is standing back amazed how brave I've been
not clinging to nostalgia's empty hand.
Anticipation makes a comeback:
the smell of lemons in a changing room;
the whisper round a soda screw-top
as an ice-cold bottle opens.

The green card corner
of the slant-cut ticket in my pocket
reassures my thumbnail.
Trains run further west from here:
this far tonight,
next time a few stops more.

The running schoolboy's coming back
towards me with that look
of timid optimism. If I could,
I'd throw a towel around his shoulders
made of better parts of memories
and set his mind at rest:
he's going to make the qualifying time
and won't do badly in the race.

Tell it Like it Might Have Been

The black car's nearside rump and flank
are pressed against the hedge.
Bindweed clinging to its bumper
and briars scratching at back wheels
seem springy with significance
enough to fill a Carlos Williams,
any-coloured, wheelbarrow.
For two days I can't pin it down –
then Wednesday begins remembering

> the van I used to clamber in,
> abandoned on an oil-soiled tussock,
> its treacly bitter sump-smell
> sweetened by the tang of lavender
> behind the taxi-driver's lock-up.
>
> Other cars in post-war black
> crouched on the verge beside the lane
> that led down to the common
> all the locals called The Lye
>
> which left the print and stain of sorrel,
> daisies, groundsel on my knees
> and joke of buttercup beneath my chin.
> Out beyond the cricket mower's circles,
> it raised itchy prickles on my back
> from bracken, yearly blackened by the fires
> scrambling from the railway cutting.
>
> Below the wood and wiremesh footbridge
> silver ribbons twitched and whispered
> as express-trains' blunt front ends
> expanded from a mile away
> to a punch of wind and warmth
> and hanging grey and yellow smells
> of vapour from the *Bournemouth Belle*.

And if those lines were quiet, sawmills
by the green canal might slice the silence –
arched distress-calls like the squealing
of the Kaplovich's pig
I thought the vet was slaughtering
when he took its rectal temperature.

Now this Wednesday inserts its question.
What's more anally retentive:
to wander off and lose myself
with an infant *alter ego*; to want
to skulk in undergrowth and blush
for having done so; or indulging
an assumption someone else might care?

Signals

I'd been going slightly crazy at each station
until the exit of the extra passengers
from our potential conversation.
Since lunchtime I'd imagined muddling up our luggage,
like a fraudster juggling ledgers, just in case
you tried to make a quick withdrawal.

Now we could talk of destinations and explore
the possibilities for supper, finding out
we'd neither of us made arrangements.

The setting sun's oblique attentions had paid off:
the clouds could not prevent a spreading orange blush
from reaching all extremities.
I felt the camber tilting us in parallel
around a right-hand curve and saw the track ahead
clear beneath an amber light.

Masquerade

I longed to tell her things about myself
to move her and amaze her, make her smile;
to get me in by stealth among her thoughts
and bring her out of hiding from my heart.

I longed to tell her things. About myself
I kept a store of fancied words I'd use –
a ring of confidences so to speak –
if conversations ever went so far.

I longed to tell her. Things about myself
prevented me from being serious
and trusting wish to words we'd drop between us.
Easy laughter's light enough to bounce.

I longed. To tell her things about myself
remained that option always in reserve;
rehearsed so often, never yet performed,
the speech with which I might bring down the house.

Close Enough for Jazz

When
    the music starts
    with just a walking bass
    and rhythm struts like melody
    till melody swings in;

When
    the beat is dancing
    round the corners of a square
    and we know that we're inside
    a tight small box together;

When
    you pull back like a sudden wave
    and leave me riding high on silence
    then double-bluff me with a shuffle
    to make a gasp rise in my throat;

And when
    I bend the string you least expect;
    or we climb a key change
    that would surely pin an audience
    to their chair backs;

Then
    our eyes engage
    and we understand again
    why lovers look at one another
    like musicians.

First Tango

Wind was bringing in the clouds
but the tide was going out
when we started dancing.
We were not on top of Beachy Head
whose edge a doomed embrace could plunge from:
our ballroom was the soft unbounded sand;
the orchestra invisible, untiring;
and angels with umbrellas
sheltered us from being drenched
in sheer implausibility.

Casting Off

The winch is labouring again
to drag a glider up to flying speed.
Its wings embrace the sky, the airflow
moaning as it passes over us.

A good strong tow into the breeze
that curls around the downs is all it needs
at first; then comes the search for updraughts
and patient winding up through warmer spirals.

Bodyheat is reassuring:
your hand in mine makes me forget to check
my instruments. We've climbed so far
relying on the tightness of excitement,

which at a certain point gets risky.
Past forty-five degrees the downward force
exceeds the forward; which is why
ground crews keep an axe available.

Norwegian Wood

Split wedge logs bake like chunks of marble cake.
Oozing resin dribbles, spits and sizzles
while small insects fail to make a getaway.

From the dancing darkness Lorraine's watching,
curled up, cosy on the vivid bedspread.
When Lennon asks if there's anybody listening
she thinks that she's the girl who's come to stay.

It's 1965 and next year, when the fire's finished,
what will happen is I'll split her heart.

Atmospheres

Gasping in that carpark under Avignon,
her face was smeared with tears to rinse the sting
of fumes that failing fans had left behind.
He was little better, but enough
to help her up a stairway to escape
the certainty she'd not survive.

They made themselves feel better with a beer
and finding fault with how the other tourists dressed.
They watched a labourer, whose broom was slower
than the breeze, try patiently to gather
fallen leaves that danced away from him,
spinning down towards October.

At a lower level, ventilation systems
had not quite dispelled the residues
of grievances arriving steadily
all through the week. But they could still remember,
how to chase and sometimes even catch
a bunch of rustling scattered dreams.

Moonlight Masquerade

An unusually full moon
projects the casement shape across the wall
at three a.m. like painted scenery.
Sleep's receding irresistibly again
as if dragged on the tide-pull
that swung *Apollo 13*, back to earth.

My unsteered memory free-falls
past sun and moon masks in a Venice workshop.
We quarrelled there because I diagnosed
a fin-de-siecle sickness in your fascination
for Punchinello smiles
and empty eyes for lies to hide behind.

Masks are for professionals:
amateur imposters miss the cues
to drop them. Paint goes brittle and the cracks
get emphasised the more a face is rubbed
in solitude as thick
as printer's ink and black as moonless night.

At the Caffé del Tasso

     I
This is where the doubles come
to drink themselves into existence.
A silver-headed Elvis, bouffant still,
is puffing a cigar and sipping
something filled with oranges
and shells; and last night there was Humphrey Bogart,
brizzolato, busy kissing fingers
of a well-heeled, not barefoot, contessa.
My grandad and a third man, draped in black,
play cards with lighter grey opponents.

     II
Where there's justice, peace and love
there's God, declares the clock across the square
in Latin. All three might be too much
to claim: but there's a sense of doing rather well
as the lady with a pretty nose
and shoulders laughs delightfully
and smoke curls past a denim waistcoat.
In a cloaked, flamboyant gesture
Tasso's statue cradles pigeons
like a stone ersatz St Francis.

     III
A woman begging breaks the spell.
Minus magic, faces freeze:
each conversation closes ranks
and solitary drinkers read their beer mats
as she moves between the tables,
the inverse of a waitress.
A passing pigeon parts my hair
as Tasso's feathered friends abandon him.
At least I turned half-way towards her
briefly as I shook my head.

      IV
In the multi-mirrored men's room
there's my twice-reflected likeness
edging in and out of vision,
never quite the way that I'd expect.
Unlike that familiar
and volte-face doppelganger
who maintains a brazen stare
above the taps, my proper self
and I are having all the usual trouble
meeting one another's gaze.

Bergamo, 2002

Killing Time at the Flying-boat Museum

Silver clippers used to gather here
and thrash along the Shannon's soft wet runway,
labouring like swans. Their web-foot sponsons
scuffed and skipped the waves until wide wings
could grudgingly begin the westward climb,
tail-heavy with official subsidies
on British mails to Ottawa and Lagos.

> When newsreel boasts of flying boats
> assume their near-Imperial importance,
> making much of Public Face comes close
> to poking fun at facing facts
> as hard as, say, a grimly private diagnosis.

Glass and aluminium nostalgia
stops at pre-war prices in the tea-room.
Past the single tables, rain-blurred windows
hint at spectres of departure: porters
walking trolleys to the ramp; the boatmen
shuttling to *Canopus*; stewards serving
canapés hand-made in tiny pantries.

> No ocean's vast catastrophe of breakers
> can make a separation bleaker
> than the distance to a few tomorrows,
> like white houses on an outstretched arm
> of land beyond a river when the bridge is gone.

Static seeps across the wireless room.
Some gramophone has finished braying *Amy,
wonderful Amy* and is scratching round
the centre of a silence as if scanning
wavebands endlessly for SOS calls,
puzzled voices from the far Atlantic
not quite loud enough to understand.

If attenuated warnings whisper
sooner than the ultimatum comes,
those signals ride unstable frequencies
that fine-tuned dials cannot fix.
Like rarest butterflies they won't be pinned to cards.

All the standard measurements will do
is mask the would-be telltale tremors
in a placid atmosphere
and guarantee a taking by surprise
as common specimens are netted for the jar.

There's just the wreck of *Echo-Sugar*'s engine
left to show for hours of fog-bound droning
waiting to come home. Meticulous
corrections for a wind that wasn't there
unpicked the holding pattern's tidy knot
unknowingly to dangling loops whose ends
were always bound to snag against a mountain.

Foynes, Co. Limerick

Loss Adjusters

They walk beside disused canals
wearing matching jackets. At the collars
slightly shiny uncut hair
has curled, untidy as an unkept promise.
Afterwards, behind uncurtained windows,
they resume a sleepless dialogue
on lists of post-disaster redesigns.

> *A strain-gauge to tell if the building is bulging;*
> *foundations dug deeper to shore up the spire;*
> *conventional spars should replace surface bracing;*
> *make fuel-chamber gaskets resistant to fire.*

Partnership or kinship means
they share a common blueprint. One's left-handed
so they sidle counter-crabwise
scavenging round tragedies.
Beyond too late, there's always time
for lodging ever-overdue objections
to tenders that should not have won the contract.

> *The signals defaulting to safe not to danger;*
> *no lightning rod earthing the main mooring mast;*
> *not enough lifeboats for all the ship's complement;*
> *the iron bridge girders imperfectly cast.*

Why make attempts to make amends
for other parties' negligence or crimes?
After blaming's had its day
in court, no praise awaits portfolios
of hindsights. Sorting *should-have-beens*,
to salvage just one *could-be*: this, they must
believe, does more than set a record straight.

> *No missing bulkheads to weaken the vessel;*
> *fill no more airships with porous gas-bags;*
> *add reinforcement at corners of windows;*
> *let cracks be acknowledged, not hidden by flags.*

So, What Happened ?

Perspiration pricked like fingernails;
and panic fisted stomach acid to the throat.
Corrosive words emerged
before a whimpering of pain which echoed
the gasping cough of something breaking.

With no black box to tell what stresses,
what manoeuvres caused (or came before) the crash,
inquiry has no choice
but let a culprit pick the culprit's face
from identikit components.

So make the nostrils not so flared;
find kinder eyes; say nothing firm about the mouth.
When taken to the line-up,
claim there is no perpetrator present
and simply indicate the stand-ins.

Party Trick

You know that thing they do –
illusionists –
with razor blades?
They swallow them
and follow with a thread and needle;
then they pull the whole lot up
all strung together.
Well that's the way the tale came out,
as separated episodes:
each rebuff,
recrimination,
insult, setback
had its own keen edges;
and each fetched up the next
with no more hesitation,
no more effort than a tug upon a twine.
This was no vomiting
of mangled fragments of mistreatment
but a drawing out
of singular
and stainless grievances,
specific and intact complaints.
The chain of sharps
made no visible incisions
in the mouth they issued from;
which subsequently
might cause an audience
to wonder what rehearsal
lay behind such sleight of tongue.

Analysis

To find that he was devious
came as a surprise to him.
The fact had tried to hide its own existence.
Keeping cards of every colour
up his sleeve, he was no sharper,
when he palmed them, than an amateur
magician needing to divert
a sympathetic audience.

He'd hardly tell himself his own opinions,
fearing he would let them slip
to someone who'd be unconvinced.
Delaying declaration of decisions
was essential for avoiding
explanations, shielding him
from blame for what he hadn't said he'd planned.

Curtain Call

They've already done
> the *old enough to be your* ... bit –
leaving out his line
> that goes, *I'm twenty on the inside.*
Happily for her,
> it's good old outside in control
(*in loco parentis*,
> or at least avuncular).
He's flirting just enough
> for him to hope he'll hear her think
I suppose he's still
> *attractive when he wants to be.*
He's flirting just enough,
> although he does not make a pass,
to remind himself
> of when he might have had that choice.

Adultery-on-Sea

He became entangled in a cliché
the moment that he started to erect
the temporary triangle. Bright colours
striped on canvas curved inviting him
to do it in dark glasses while the sun shone
with *Kiss Me Quick* pulled down across his face.

The strength of his position hung upon
the gap between two frames of reference
remaining fixed as Euclid's propositions:
when one prop failed his situation folded
with the weight of evidence and caught him
by his short and curly fingers. Bang
to rights, he still got off by playing on
compassion for a self-made stretcher case.

Denunciation

When you wrote
from Iowa about black wings,
one low, one curving
like a scythe, you could have said
the downswept point
was either feathering a blessing
or fingering adultery.
I knew which one you'd choose.

It amused you
when that human-glider hybrid
was assembled
on a hillside over Gateshead;
you admired,
in Tampere, the stretcher-case
from Simberg's imagination
brought down to earth by urchins.

Authentic angels
are the kind you don't have time for –
Renaissance ones,
androgynous and dignified
on *terra firma*;
implausible as bumble bees,
on grounds of ergonomics,
as soon as they get airborne.

How odd that painters,
who really did believe the church
told truths that lie
beyond their canvases and frescoes,
should leave behind
these likenesses of messengers
that help you disbelieve
there ever was a message.

Voice

Once, when I was biking home from school,
a proper cyclist overtook me
and the shelter of his slipstream
let me hope of going faster
than I could. For five amazing minutes
I kept up – though never passed him –
pedals making no resistance
in that highest gear as I achieved
a speed I'd been designed for after all.

Which is how it feels as words
bunch up and press like muscles striving
for momentum. It's a chase
to catch and capture axioms
which state there really is a way
to fail to dwell on pain that's been
and gone, a way to skip recriminations
and – instead of what dead people
did and didn't get the blame for –
make the point be who's alive
not what becomes – became – of whose remains.

Fault Lines

Most of us
will always hate you – all of you –
because
we know that some of yours
have done away with some of ours.
And though a few of us
have paid too few of you
in blood
it's nowhere near enough
for any one of us
to start forgetting
what there is to hold against
those of you still left.

Each last one of you,
whatever you pretend,
knows you'd really like
to wipe out all of us:
but only some of us
will come right out and say so.
And now there's one or two
among us going soft:
they want to let you off –
the lot of you –
for all the things
the rest of us will find a way
to settle with you for, one day.

So first we'll deal with them.

Tribe

We are children of the wind.
We travel gently on our mother's arm
keep rhythm with her breath
and murmured song.
Only when we must, we hasten
proud, emboldened
by our father's open-throated roar.

We are brothers to the sand.
Being many, we can claim a space
and hold it by our shifting
weight of numbers.
Our feet tread lightly, make no prints
to walk behind us:
owning all, we leave the landscape empty.

We are not alone.
Those others
always haunt the corners of our eyes
but at a distance, where we try to keep them.
They have tried to tighten borders round us.

They are made of mud
and dung;
are pale, soft-skinned and have short-sighted eyes;
consume spiced rotting foods, not fresh tough meat;
and crouch confined in one another's smells.

Their dwellings foul the ground,
like droppings
left to dry. They hide their sluggish, heavy
bodies from the sun and cold. Their minds
inhabit worlds where words change shape like dunes.

We lay no lines
across the pure and proper curves of earth.
We borrow ground while they
relinquish none
of what they occupy *as well*
and not *instead*.
If we meet, we meet as enemies.

Clips of Documentary Footage

Slow mist rolling like a wave across a field
breaks and shows where frozen furrows keep
the shape of earth that might have promised greenery and growth
now closed against the plough that runs too deep.

Dumb animals in tests, it's said,
can learn a language,
if they're taken time and time enough
down mazes made to make a point.
Perhaps. But then we must allow
they might just want to signal
an urgent wish to finish, be elsewhere.

Slow smoke blowing like a veil across a face
whose lines reveal that sorrow doesn't sleep;
his frozen mouth is softened by no memory of mirth
and closed against the plea that runs too deep.

Dismissing us and it, he says
it's of no interest,
not worth talking any more about
dead people in a long-time past.
Untrue. But still we can't deny
his right to his denial,
earned by having far too much to tell.

Their Minds Were Settled

Their minds were settled as they went on board
with one-way tickets – more than they would need.
Six dozen virgins each seemed fair reward.

One purpose bound them tightly like a cord.
With wooden faces no-one else could read
their minds were settled as they went on board

believing that the heavens would applaud
their private holy war surprise attack.
Six dozen virgins each seemed fair reward.

Fierce obsession easily ignored
the screams of panic. They would not turn back:
their minds were settled as they went on board.

And all were dead as burning jet-fuel poured
through buildings folding under their own weight.
Six dozen virgins each seemed fair reward.

Those undetected Stanley-knives have scored
the calendar, that unsuspecting date.
Six dozen virgins each seemed fair reward;
their minds were settled as they went on board.

Foreboding

In Wurzburg once, on business and between appointments,
a guidebook took me looking for the Ancient Crane.
Its icon on my map was out-of-scale and triggered
inward cowering against its dark and crooked
presence looming up above me like a beak
as sudden and as awful as the bulk that shocked
my childhood's eye, high-stranded at a street's end, stuck
on slick Thames mud. That Essex coaster – hardly vast –
was appalling out of all proportion.

On one of several days alone in Islington
I met a man whose broken accent matched the life
he had to reconcile with wife and children's deaths.
Xeroxed in my head's a picture that he showed:
a JCB is squatting in a market place;
its filthy single arm, hydraulically elbowed,
works a batch of puppets from a six-branched hanger
for an audience who've been compelled to watch them
jerk and choke into oblivion.

A fact is sometimes small and made of wood and sometimes
built from brutal iron ribs. Our fears will seize on
scraps left over when a thing no-one should ever
have to face has finished happening – then weld them
to that metal skeleton we first assembled,
growing up, to represent all nameless dreads.
That huge and ugly hull still hovers hellishly
to crush or drown us. We board it in the certainty
we're never coming back from where it's going.

Capital Offence

Great-great-grandad's execution passed off pretty messily:
roped and choking, kicking legs protesting
to a jeering jury cheering his extinction
in a bear-pit stink.

Two great-uncles were turned off more or less in privacy,
ankle-strapped in limewashed premises:
one heavy-gauge electric switch; one well-oiled trap,
abattoir-efficient.

(A less distressing process was adopted by authorities
when middle-class distaste for block or scaffold
meant that fewer swing votes hung on playing up
convicted siblings' pain.)

A Texan second kissing-cousin was put down rather daintily
by needle with a vet's detachment
and a padded armrest, while shock-resistant glass
cushioned the spectators.

More distant relatives turn up with internet immediacy
on makeshift gibbets, videoed beheadings.
In a stadium, a crowd applauds to match
the clapping of machine guns.

And sometimes even far-off kin are treated as close family –
like Cain, not put to death but put on unmarked
planes to unreal lands, whose dust keeps any blood
from spattering our shoes.

Cover-up

Draw the curtains over Guernica.
On no account remember screaming horses,
let alone the howling mouths of children
and their mothers when the borrowed bombers
loomed and plunged. Too much illumination
here; the hand-clasped oil lamp; the flames;
a single filament still glowing as
the ceiling's falling. How can broken swordsmen
brandish pointed tongues at cameras
underneath that bloody naked bulb?

Fool's-errand Boys

Who do they think they're fooling, purveyors
of government bluff? Do they somehow suppose
you sound more grown-up the more cant you bray as
you keep pissing yourself for fear of who'll hurt you
for each line you muff? Or that, if they only chose,
they could alter things back to when they slept at night
or had their own visions or joined arms with real virtue?
Or do they fancy there's really been no change
and that they've always believed that black could just as well
                                                          be white,
or sat through days of mean and weasel scheming
watching lies ooze? If they don't (and they can't), it's strange:
                                        why aren't they screaming?

Perhaps to be hired you must have little room
inside your head for empathy or being bold
as prompters hiss at you to preach what they assume,
deny all harms then vomit slimy care
for victims. Would they balk at being told
to walk on water? Promotions keep them quiet:
the stumbling blocks so obvious from elsewhere
for them are stepping stones. Can they never smell
what's gagging them, what makes them claim that they
                                          were right
(at worst, were misinformed)? Never throughout
their sweaty introverted public lives? Well,
                                      they'll get found out

after Philip Larkin's "The Old Fools"

To Whom it May Concern

When I heard the way they'd treated you
I wanted, very calmly,
to crush my glass against the table top.

And that would testify
I hadn't anything to do with them –
not the border clerks
who fingered through your papers,
nor the authors of their picklock questions,
shaped to make the wrong replies slide out
like bolts drawn slowly back across a trapdoor.

I wanted to shout down their smug assumption
of my mute agreement
to brand you, steal your clothes and make you dance.

Denials alone won't do
for those who make their own small ugly choices.
I needed, very simply,
to know if God could answer
the question of how far the likes of us
should take an inkling of complicity
when we remember how they treated you.

Troubadours

A dove blurts broken Morse along the breeze:
a *m'aidez* out of time deprived of rest
by ducal talons poised above the trees
and cuckoo henchmen plundering the nest.
Princelings making playthings of these gardens
struck up cheap rapports with balladeers:
when Honour mattered more than honest tears
laments for murdered scions could win pardons.

We too can live like lords: expect unseen
somebody else to mop away our wastes,
to kill our meat and leave our fingers clean;
and in bastides we give some self-preserving
enterprisers free play with our tastes.
They strum on us the tunes we're well-deserving.

Notes

The Otters Greet St Cuthbert
When St Cuthbert visited Coldingham Priory he spent a night in prayer, standing in the sea. As he came out of the water a pair of sea-otters attached themselves to his feet and would not leave until he gave them his blessing.

Stained Glass in Tudeley Church
All Saints Church in Tudeley, Kent has twelve stained glass memorial windows by Marc Chagall.

Jairus
Mark 5:35-43

Moonlight Masquerade
The Apollo 13 lunar mission suffered severe technical problems and its safe return was achieved using an improvised slingshot manoeuvre round the moon.

Denunciation
According to legend, the Black Angel in Oakland Cemetery, Iowa, turned black as a reminder of unfaithfulness by a dead spouse. Antony Gormley's sculpture *Angel of the North* overlooks the A1 motorway at Gateshead. Hugo Simberg's painting *The Wounded Angel* is in Tampere Cathedral, Finland.

Cover-up
In February 2003 the reproduction of Picasso's painting *Guernica* at the UN headquarters in New York was curtained over during press briefings which followed Security Council debates on Iraq.